CW01020468

Copyright 2013

Daniel Jordano

THE BEST BOOK ON ACTING

How to become a better actor instantly--

without killing yourself with the "Method"

Discover the psychological secrets of the "LIFE ACTING System"

Table of Contents

INTRODUCTION

When you think of the acting performances that have inspired you, I wager that they were the ones where the actor was so focused, so alive, so in tune with his or her desires, that you were enraptured. They quickened your pulse--made you laugh. They affected you. Even in the so-called "quiet moments", it was the actor's thoughts-- which somehow you could "read"-- that kept you riveted. This is the height of good acting. It doesn't get any better than this.

Of course, there is a history of the dramatic arts. We can see by the popular styles of acting over the years, what that history was influenced by. For history itself is not an accident. History is the working out of the thoughts of men. It is this "working out" of the philosophies of the times that have influenced our aesthetics or theory of art. Not understanding this fact has kept us in the dark, and has been a source of our aesthetic problems. Aesthetic styles are the outworking of a deeper philosophy-- of one's metaphysics, epistemology, ethics, and politics. These all overlap and contribute to the resulting aesthetics of the day.

> **Aesthetic styles are the outworking of the Philosophy of the Times.**

Let me illustrate from film history. Simply looking at the

history of acting in the medium of film, we can see how culture and philosophy affected film acting. For instance, at the turn of the century (technologically speaking) the medium was in its infancy and had not developed sound. Visuals were king. Acting styles were being adapted from the stage. Therefore, the acting styles were more demonstrative, more ostentatious, just as the first decade of the 20th century was. It was a decade of invention, of innovation, of glamour and wealth, excess, and luxury.

Is it an accident that these themes also affected the style of acting at this time? Of course not! There is always a dialectic functioning between the themes of the times and the styles of the times. This can be vividly seen in every new style of film since then.

For example, can anyone deny that the post-war ethos of cynicism (in light of the millions slain in WW2) directly affected and led to an aesthetic of skepticism, darkness, and moral ambiguity? - And that this ethos led to the style of Film Noir, and also to an edgier style of acting?

Later, the great films of Italian Neo-Realism came out of a desire to be more truthful about the horrifically challenging social issues of the day. This movement contributed to the casting of what they called (incorrectly, in my opinion) non-actors. Of course, the performances by the so-called "non-actors" could be every bit as powerful as the professionally trained--sometimes, more so.

The point I am making is that the prevailing philosophies of the time impacted the styles of acting. This is natural, and will always be so. When we acknowledge this, we have to also acknowledge that any opinion which claims that a certain style is, "better", can only be opinion-- anything more is simply fanaticism.

Unfortunately, we have been duped as artists from an early age, especially in the theatrical arts, that there is a "right" way of doing things. We have our devotees of Stanislavsky, Lee Strasberg, and the Actors Studio and the Method, Stella Adler, or David Mamet, or Sanford Meisner. We argue with one another rather than looking deeper, rather than looking at the philosophical presuppositions of these schools. Remember: the results of these schools are simply the manifestation of the philosophical presuppositions of their teachers. For example, Meisner thought Strasberg was too internally focused. Robert Lewis thought most method actors were neglectful of style, and so on.

Similarly, my philosophy of acting derives from my understanding of the nature of man, and the way he views the world. This understanding is derived from fairly recent studies in behavioral psychology.

PHILOSOPHY OF LIFE ACTING

My philosophy of dramatic arts, I call LIFE ACTING.

1) LIFE ACTING- sees the goal of the performer as the complete focus on the IMMEDIATE LIFE of the character. Life is the actual dynamic that is happening in the present. It is very present focused.

Therefore, the priority of LIFE ACTING is never contextual. LIFE ACTING is never as concerned with characterization, accents, makeup, wardrobe, projection, blocking, marks, etc. Theses things have their place, but they are NOT acting. They are simply choices made in homework. Homework is homework and acting is acting.

Unfortunately, we haven't learned that way. We have given contextual issues as much weight as situational issues, and the tension between the two has been an albatross around our collective necks!

A NEW PHILOSOPHY

It is the point of LIFE ACTING to free the performer. This freedom is not based on whim or arbitrary style, but on a new and very specific philosophy of the human being. In fact, it is my contention that solid grounding in the philosophy of humanity (anthropology) including psychology, is of the utmost importance in the dramatic arts. Why? Simply because it is what we believe about men and women and how they function in the world that will most influence our choices as actors

> **It is what we believe about men and women and how they function in the world that will most influence our choices as actors.**

In this short primer, I will present the basics of this new philosophy of acting. Chapter 1 will deal with psychological research and discoveries that have influenced our understanding of the way men think. Chapter 2 will explain how these discoveries have impacted our view of humanity in general. In Chapter 3, we will look at how these understandings radically affect our view of the acting process and goals. I know you might be tempted to go right to this chapter. Try to resist, because the first two chapters are the keys to understanding Chapter 3. In Chapter 4, we will look at "Characterization", what does it mean and how do we do it? Finally, in Chapter 5, I will describe some exercises that are especially important for the actor's instrument.

CHAPTER 1
THE PSYCHOLOGY OF ACTING

Behaviorism is an approach to psychology that emerged in the early 20th century. It's primary tenet, as expressed in the writing of B.F. Skinner and others, is that psychology should concern itself with the observable behavior of people, not with unobservable events that take place in their minds. Behaviorism emerged as a reaction to the more internal or "mentalistic" philosophies of the time.

On the other hand, Stanislavsky and the later method teachers were heavily influenced by Freud and the psychoanalytic movement, which focuses on childhood events, irrational, unconscious drives, and bringing these unconscious drives into consciousness in order to deal with them. One of the key principles of the Stanislavsky "system' was his use of "affective memory", which requires actors to call on the personal memories of past events that are similar to what their character is experiencing. Lee Strasberg later developed "sense memory" as the recall of physical sensations surrounding a past event, in order to draw out the emotions involved with that event.

The philosophy I will be advocating relies much more on the behaviorist tradition, than in the Freudian tradition, which will become clear. One reason that I favor the behaviorist tradition is its emphasis on observable phenomena.

LIFE ACTING contends that man is basically an aspirational creature with LIFE as his consuming goal. How do we claim this? By making observations of how man lives in the world. From the time of birth, it can be observed that the human infant has needs and desires. It finds itself thrust from the relative security of the womb, into a hostile environment. It becomes quickly aware that its LIFE wants to be maintained. It senses its need for warmth, for touch, for air, for food, and for drink. It fights for these needs primarily through crying. Even though a human infant is probably the most helpless creature on earth, it bursts with LIFE and with a passion to LIVE! How does it live? ---By getting its needs met. How does it get its needs met? ----Passion!

This is the human drama from cradle to grave.

> # LIFE ACTING contends that man is basically an aspirational creature with
> # LIFE as his consuming goal.

So what do we observe of mankind? - That from cradle to grave man is a self-interested being. He is interested in keeping himself alive, attaining his dreams, longing for affection, approval, friendship, love, esteem, money, sex, fame, etc.

Why is it so important to see man like this? Because that is the way he is! The closer our philosophy aligns with our observations the better. Several psychological studies bear witness to this presupposition.

COGNITIVE DISSONANCE

Cognitive Dissonance is the feeling of discomfort when simultaneously holding two or more conflicting ideas. Leon Festinger, who chronicled the followers of a UFO cult as reality clashed with their belief in an impending alien-caused apocalypse, coined the term. (Festinger, 1956) When the prophesied time came, and no apocalypse with it, the followers faced serious "cognitive dissonance". Were they a victim of a hoax? The cult had a strong motivational desire to reduce this discomfort.

Rather than accept the idea that their cult was bogus, the majority of the cult members (who had sold all their possessions) accepted the theory that the aliens had given them a second chance and increased their proselytization fervently.

The principle is that one of the deep needs of man is to align his beliefs and to eliminate cognitive dissonance. When faced with certain facts, his capacity to rationalize in order to avoid dissonance is astonishing.

A classic illustration is Aesop's fable, *The Fox and the Grapes*. In the story, a fox sees some high hanging grapes, and wishes to eat them. When the fox can't think of a way to attain them, he decides the grapes are not worth eating. He justifies his lack of effort to reduce dissonance.

Jack Brehm did an experiment where 225 female students were asked to rate a series of common appliances, and were allowed to take two of them home as gifts. (Brehm, 1956)When the ratings were done again, the women rated the brands they took home higher than before. In other words, the women justified the choice they had made.

People have a need to seek consonance, or agreement and harmony between their expectations and reality. When dissonance occurs, they tend to try to reduce it in three ways: lowering the importance of one of the factors, (like the fox in the fable), adding consonant elements (like the aliens giving the cult a second chance) or changing one of the dissonant factors.

All this leads us to the principle that people's beliefs are quite often not based on scientifically proven facts, but are held in order to minimize cognitive dissonance. In other words our beliefs are often held sheerly to justify our decisions to ourselves!

> **Our beliefs are often held sheerly to justify our decisions to ourselves!**

Let's put this in another way: **we tend to believe in the things we have done simply because we have done them**, regardless of the wisdom, soundness, or rightness of those choices.

13

When we grasp this element of human nature then we can understand a Napoleon, a Macbeth, or even a John Dillinger.

Norman Vincent Peale, in his book, *How to Win Friends and Influence People*, recalled the incident of Two-Gun Crowley, a convicted cop killer, who on the way to the electric chair said, "This is what I get for defending myself". The point being that people hardly ever blame themselves for anything. We will be looking at the implications of this later.

CONTEXT IS KING

The famous Milgram experiment measured the willingness of volunteers to administer painful electric shocks to a "patient", by the prompting of an authority figure. (Milgram, 1963) The "patient" was (unbeknownst to the volunteer) just pretending to be horrifically shocked when answering questions incorrectly. Separated by a wall, even the screams of pain from the "patient" were not enough to stop the volunteers from administering what they thought might even be fatal electric shocks, while gently prodded by the authority figure supervising the proceedings. 65 percent of the volunteers administered the experiment's final 450-volt shock. This experiment gave an appreciation of the power that a structured, authoritative context can have on people's justification of their actions.

The theatrical endeavor also can be a highly structured environment. The contextual factors can be very powerful indeed. Understanding that we come to believe, or rationalize the things we do is a powerful ally to the actor.

> **We come to believe in the things we are doing, regardless of why we started doing them.**

ACTOR- OBSERVER BIAS

Actor – observer bias (Jones & Nisbett, 1971) is the theory that when a person judges their own behavior, they are more likely to attribute their actions to the particular situation than to a generalization about their personality. Yet when judging the actions of another, thus becoming an "observer", people are more likely to attribute behavior to a person's overall disposition, not situational factors. This tendency was examined in an experiment where volunteers were asked to "rate" various people according to a scale of character traits. The people included themselves. They could also select "depends on situation". The results showed that the volunteers used the "depends on situation" option only for themselves. People tend to view themselves as fluid and others as "characters" with distinct personality traits.

> **People tend to view themselves as fluid and others as "characters".**

A later reformulation of the theory found that those judging their own behavior, offer more "reason explanations" for what they do, whereas, when they judge others, as observers, they tend to offer more "belief" or "desire" explanations for why others act. In other words, when I do something, I call it reasonable, but when you do something, I tend to say it's because of what you believe or desire. This is the human tendency. Psychological experiments continue to make the case that human beings are extremely egocentric.

Psychological experiments continue to make the case that human beings are extremely egocentric.

SELF-SERVING BIAS

The "self-serving bias" refers to individuals attributing their success to internal personal factors, but attributing their failures to external or situational factors. This bias is a mechanism for people to protect their self-esteem. In experiments conducted by Wolosin, Sherman and Till, participants had to choose among geographic locations where they thought they were most likely to meet a friend. (Wolosin, Sherman and Till, 1973) They performed this task in competition, both individually, and with a partner. When receiving positive feedback, in the cooperative case, they assumed more responsibility than their partner. The partner was assigned more responsibility in failure outcomes. In the individual scenario, participants took more responsibility for positive outcomes and blamed situational factors for negative outcomes.

These scientific studies are very important in understanding individual's egocentricity. For the actor, these become doubly important, as we shall examine.

CHAPTER 2
PHILOSOPHY OF MAN

Philosophy is a way of looking at the world. It is a belief about the way the world works. A philosophy of life is held by all of us, even if we are not conscious of it. Aesthetics is the branch of philosophy that has to do with the arts. But it does not stand by itself. Our philosophy of art is based on our views of the other branches of philosophy: Metaphysics, Epistemology, Ethics, and Politics. The more consistent that our views align, the more logical and consistent we are in our lives. The truth is we are all a mixed bag of contradictions.

As it pertains to acting, it is of great importance to understand what we believe about the nature of man. (Anthropology)

LIFE ACTING contends that man is basically an aspirational creature with LIFE as his consuming goal.

GOOD AND BAD

Based on the psychological studies in the last chapter, our philosophy of man is that man is an incredibly egocentric creature. One might call this self centered or selfish. This selfishness has been decried in some theologies as evil. But is that the case? Do we call animals selfish for desiring to keep themselves alive? No, it merely makes sense from the standpoint of existence. But we don't even give man that much credit. I prefer to use the term "reasonable self-interest" because the term "selfishness" has come to mean a blatant disregard for the welfare of others.

> **It is an undue emphasis on "good or bad", regarding the characters we play that leads to so many safe and passionless choices in our approach as actors.**

As regards to whether this self-interest is good or bad, we need not concern ourselves, as it pertains to the dramatic arts. In fact, it is an undue emphasis on "good or bad", regarding the characters we play, that lead to so many safe and passionless choices in our approach as actors. We must de-emphasize questions of good and bad and just observe what is. We must stop judging our characters!

REASON AND VOLITION

Man, in keeping himself alive, finds that he must use something which the animals do not possess but which he needs: his mind and his ability to reason. In addition, it becomes clear that man possesses a free will.

Man has:

1. An ability to reason
2. Volition or self-determination

These abilities inherent in man, unlike other creatures, are absolutely necessary for his survival. He can ignore reason to his own peril. But his volition and his reason make possible the choice of values. Now in order to make man a moral being he must have these qualities. He must have reason, he must have knowledge and he must have a free will. As actors we must take these faculties very seriously.

> ## Our thoughts are key to controlling our emotions and behaviors.

As we have seen from our psychological studies, our thoughts are key to controlling our emotions and behaviors, and our volition makes it possible to often choose our beliefs. We will often choose our beliefs based on the emotional benefit they give to us. This makes our thoughts and beliefs very important to us and more specifically to the characters we play as actors.

> ## We will often use our volition to choose beliefs based on the emotional benefit they give us!

Secondly, based on the previous chapter, we see that the psychological experiments described there, make no sense unless the individuals in those studies had freedom to choose their responses.

Now we may debate the level of freedom, but nevertheless, there is at least the illusion of freedom to the mind of the individual.

VALUES

One of the chief ways we use our volition as people is to choose our values. This is what makes us who we are. Though our values may have come to us culturally, in the end, we decide whether to embrace or reject every value we have. This is important for us, and important in the creation of our characters-- as we shall see.

> **Man is a self-interested creature. Man's emotional life is as important, and often more important to him, than any other need.**

This is a very cursory look at the nature of man. No matter what you might believe about whether man possesses a soul, or whether he is born with an evil nature, we can agree, based on psychological research on the following:

Man is a self-interested creature. In order to further his self-interest and survival, he has the ability to reason, and to choose. Using these abilities enable man to choose his thoughts and values, which directly affect his emotional life. Man's emotional life is as important, and often more important to him, than any other need.

CHAPTER 3
LIFE ACTING: EGOCENTRICITY

LIFE ACTING is revelatory in the sense that it is based on the previous psychological findings and a resulting specific philosophy of man. How do these affect the practice of acting? The following is a summary of the LIFE ACTING process.

EGOCENTRICITY

One thing revealed in the research is the natural egocentricity of individuals. In other words, people are concerned with themselves and their situations primarily and predominately. This must be true of the characters we portray. LIFE ACTING is committed to the complete egocentricity of the characters we play.

> **LIFE ACTING is committed to the complete egocentricity of the characters we play.**

Our characters must focus on their present situation, not on their own personality! This is so simple and yet so profound. This is the core of LIFE ACTING.

CONCENTRATION ON THE SITUATION

If the situation should be the focus of the actor, we find that when the actor is fully there, giving and responding in a genuine way, that there is a fascination, a delight, and an interest in the performance, on the part the audience.

> **Our characters must focus on their present situation, not on their own personality! This is the core of LIFE ACTING.**

Now does this mean that our focus is so much on the situation that we suppress, ignore or deny the contextual factors like audience and camera etc.? Absolutely not! Our concentration must include these environmental contexts. We will examine this in the next chapter.

PURPOSE

Another core principle of LIFE ACTING is that there MUST be a purpose and intent behind every action of the performer. The actor must pursue victory of purpose. This is really all there is to it. The intent must be communicated to the audience. Isn't it so that when you don't understand the intent of the actor, that the scene can become flat and boring? Of course! It's as flat and boring as a quarterback reading the newspaper after the snap of the football!

> **Another core principle of LIFE ACTING is that there MUST be a purpose and intent behind every action of the performer.**

From our studies of psychology and philosophy, we understand that there is a drive of every creature to sustain and better its life. This is the LIFE that we are after in LIFE ACTING! Life is a force. This is a force that demands to be released, demands to be embraced, and demands to be expressed.

It is easy to dismiss the goals of characters. When we start doing this though, we have begun to judge the character from the outside, and have distanced ourselves from his own egocentricity. We will then begin to play a caricature--a cartoon. If we want real LIFE, we must commit to staying "inside" the character, playing his own egocentricity in his situation, with all his rationalizations etc.

Will you play Adolph Hitler as a monster-- as a caricature? Or will you realize that he had a way to rationalize, justify and rid his mind of all the cognitive dissonance created by his actions? Only when you choose the latter will the character come to life.

FUTURE ORIENTATION

The complete focus of the actor on his intentions means at any given moment, he is future oriented. That means at the time of performance the actor is not thinking about the past, his character, personality, but pressing in to his desired future.

> **IN LIFE ACTING, we don't discuss "motivation", but only what is the current <u>intention</u>.**

Many of us actors are used to discussing characters in terms of "motivation", as in what is instigating, or causing this action. This word is past oriented, in the sense that we are looking for something from the past, which is "pushing" us to the next thing. This is unhelpful, for if the actor is "future oriented", he is not so much being "pushed by the past", as being "pulled by his ideal future". In LIFE ACTING, we don't discuss motivation, but only what is the current intention. What is pulling you? The actor who keeps asking, "what's my motivation?" needs to stop thinking deterministically, and start thinking futuristically! What does my character want right now!

FEEDBACK LOOP AND THE OTHER ACTORS

In the pursuit of his goals, the actor comes to the realization that it is the other characters than can move him forward and grant him his ideal future. It is the connection with the other actors that makes the moments electric. For it is the give and takethat makes for the excitement, just as in a basketball game, it is the interplay of the teams that makes the game exciting.

Therefore, the actor must strive to be in a full contact feedback loop with the other actors. The feedback loop is a constant sending of signals, only to receive a response, and then to make immediate adjustments, and once again to attempt to achieve ones intention.

In order to do this, the actor must be committed and immersed in the feedback loop. He must have his concentration on perceiving the signals from the other actors. Without listening effectively, there is no acting!

The feedback loop is only as good as messages are received, and communications adjusted accordingly. Remember: the lines do not necessarily communicate the intentions of the character. The intentions, focus, and defining of the relationships are decided by the actor in the moment!

> **IN LIFE ACTING, the actor must strive to be in a full contact feedback loop with the other actors.**

The director and writer of course contribute to this direction. But in the moment of performance, it is the ACTOR who is listening, striving, adjusting, expressing, etc. Never forget that! The actor is the one who has the audience in his palm as he lets them into his emotional world.

LINES DON'T MAKE RELATIONSHIP

As psychological studies and experience shows, the communication of feelings is mostly a non-verbal affair. Yet, as actors we rely so much on the lines. Yes the lines are important, but the lines are just clues to what the scene is about--they are not the scenes. The scene is not the lines, but the spectacle of people trying to influence each other toward their ideal future. Knowing the lines is not acting—it's homework! There will be more on this later.

THE EMOTIONAL LIFE

The emotional life of the character is always a major concern of the actor. Because of this, many actors have placed an undue emphasis on the expression of them. Remember, in real life people are not attentive to their emotions. Emotions are responders. Emotions respond to thoughts. Therefore in the moment, the intentional thought life of the actor is always the priority. Our inclination to show our emotion often results in an ugly overacting and artificiality that is easily spotted by the audience.

Yet, emotions ARE very important to the character, as a GOAL, not so much in the moment. In LIFE ACTING we emphasize emotion in the super-objective of the character. In other words the goals or purposes of the character must be strongly emotional for the actor.

Remember in life we are usually doing our best to show little emotion. On the other hand as actors we often try to push or force the emotion. In LIFE ACTING we don't focus on emotion, we focus on the intent of the character. If the emotion is not there or strong enough, then the intent is usually not strong enough.

> **IN LIFE ACTING, we don't focus on present emotion,**
> **we focus on the emotional intent of the character. If the emotional life is lacking, usually, the intentional choices are lacking.**

Remember, many times where great vulnerability is called for; we try to hide our emotions. It is the same for our characters. Playing the physiology of trying to STOP the tears, trying to KEEP control, the body can be tricked into releasing tears. But remember to justify even the suppression of emotion by the character.

What makes a great actor great is that they are so emotionally AVAILABLE to begin with. Where most people spend their lives trying to hide their feelings, actors are trained to make them available, to put them on the surface. Exercises can help develop an emotionally available instrument, but it is the attention to the thought life of the character that will make the emotional life impactful.

IMPACTFUL CHOICES

What is it that takes a scene and makes it into artistry? It is the impact that a scene has! What gives a scene its impact? It is the amount of emotional interest we have as an audience in the scene. Therefore, one of the goals of LIFE ACTING is to develop every performance for maximum impact. How do we develop this impact as actors? It is by making the most interesting choices when it comes to intentions, tactics, internal conflicts, place, interest etc.

In LIFE ACTING, every performance is to be developed for maximum impact through interesting choices!

SIMPLICITY

In considering the above, one of the wonderful things about LIFE ACTING is the simplicity of its instruction. The actor's job can be summed up in one question. With two parts:

What do you want from the other actor and how are you going to get it?

LIFE ACTING can be summed up thus: WHAT do you want from the other actor and HOW are you going to get it?

That's it. That's our secret. That's our totality of acting. For in that one question you can be very simple but you can also go as deep as you need to.

CHAPTER 4
CONTEXT AND CHARACTERIZATION

The previous chapter gave a good summation and overview about what LIFE ACTING is all about. Now, how to do it!

ALL OF LIFE IS A PERFORMANCE

One of the most confusing things in the dramatic arts is the dichotomy placed on the actor, between thinking the thoughts of the character, and "being heard in the back row"-- the technical craft of acting.

One of the principles of LIFE ACTING is that all of life is a performance. When you are in an argument and there is a party observing, watch how your argument changes! Not only are you trying to "win" the argument, but you are also trying to make an ally of the observer-- to get him on your side! When you think about it, there is an element of this in every real life encounter.

> **In LIFE ACTING, all of LIFE is a performance. It may be God, or your own conscience but there is always an audience.**

Even if a man is at home alone fighting with his wife,

one might say that the husband's own conscience is the audience. Remember in every disagreement, there is this element of rationalization, of convincing oneself of the rightness of his cause. If one is religious, one might say God is an audience, even in the midst of the most private moments. Does the presence of an audience affect how you will act? You bet it does! BUT THERE IS ALWAYS AN AUDIENCE!

THE FOURTH WALL IS DOWN

One expression that I loathe is "the fourth wall". Many of us were taught that the "fourth wall" is the imaginary wall at the front of the stage in a traditional three walled, box set, through which the audience sees the action of the play. We learned that its presence was necessary for the "suspension of disbelief" between a fictional work and the audience, allowing them to enjoy fiction as if they were observing real events. We are taught to observe this rule. This monstrous concept has led to a host of problems, not the least of which is a false dichotomy between "living the life of the character" and "being heard in the back row".

The doctrine of the "fourth wall" has made us afraid of the audience. The audience has become our adversary. Our excuse is that we must not let the audience see any artifice. We must fool them. We must be "real", so we ignore them. The "fourth wall" has alienated us from the camera and from our audiences. That is why it must be done away with as a concept.

In its place, LIFE ACTING embraces the audience and the camera as an ally. It neither pretends the audience does not exist, nor is intimidated by its judgments. LIFE ACTING accepts that there is always an audience to be wooed, to be convinced, and to be made an ally. For example, if I am Romeo trying to convince Juliet of my love, I will have no problem "being heard in the back row", if I accept that the guy in the back row is watching and needs to be on my side!

> **LIFE ACTING rejects the "Fourth Wall" and embraces the audience or the camera, as an ally to be won over.**

It seems silly to say this. Every actor is obviously aware that there is an audience when he is on stage, or that there is a camera and make up artist five feet away from him as he performs a poignant scene. But many of us are told to ignore these things, or to try to relax in spite of their presence. LIFE ACTING does neither, but says to embrace them, use them, and win them over. The Fourth wall is down! Long Live the Revolution! When we embrace the audience, we eliminate a whole source of tension, anxiety, and conflict within the actor.

Acting for many of us has become about how well we can juggle the balls of "character", "performance technique" etc., and has become too complicated. We need to simplify. That is what LIFE ACTING is all about. The best acting is simple acting. **Most actors**

are thinking about too many things. What should we be thinking about? It's NOT about integration; it's about <u>elimination</u> and focus! We should be thinking about one thing: what does my character want from the other actors right now? That's it! How do we do this? By making a huge distinction between two things, performance and homework.

PERFORMANCE AND HOMEWORK

The process of theatrical performance consists of two things: homework and performance. Just about all the work of characterization is done in homework. Homework is more important than rehearsal in my humble opinion. Why? Because homework is where you really get to think through the worldview, intentions, and tactics of your character. Rehearsal is primarily a feedback loop where you tweak and refine with the director and other actors. What are you tweaking? What you have planned in homework.

Homework is where you really get to think through the worldview, intentions, and tactics of your character.

The most important question in homework is the summation of LIFE ACTING - "What do you want from the other actors, and how will you get it?" The beauty is that this question can be as simple or as deep as you want it to be.

WHAT DO YOU WANT FROM THE OTHER ACTOR/CHARACTER?

Why is this an important question? When you begin to define what the character wants, it speaks to his values- who the character is. When you see the other characters as being those that can give you what you want, it gives you intense focus on the other actors in the play. It makes you think through every relationship very carefully and thoroughly.

As we learned in our psychological studies, every other actor in the play should be "characterized" in terms of what they can do for you.

Following is an example of all the homework you can do by just answering the one question from LIFE ACTING with different emphasis on each part of the sentence.

1) **WHAT** do you want? What is the objective of this character? What is his super-objective? What are his sub-objectives in every scene, every line?

2) What do **YOU** want? - What do clues from the script say about the personality of your character? What is your character's worldview? How does he see the other characters and how does he feel about them?

3) What do you **WANT**? Is your objective strong enough? Interesting enough?

4) **FROM** the other actors/characters- how can the other actors

give you what you want?

5) From the other **ACTORS/CHARACTERS**- who are the other actor/characters? How do they feel about you? What do they want from you? How do you feel about them?

...AND HOW ARE YOU GOING TO GET IT?

6) **HOW** are you going to get it? What tactics will you use to achieve your super-objective and sub-objectives in every line? Varied? Interesting? Imaginative?

7) How are **YOU** going to get it? What props, dress, movement, speech, makeup, would YOUR character use that would communicate his personality but also further his objective?

8) How are you going to **GET** it? Are you expecting to win, pressing in to your ideal future?

There really is no point of presenting a scene or monologue for rehearsal without doing a preliminary answer to these questions. The problem in many scene study groups or classes is that many of the actors JUST HAVEN'T DONE THEIR HOMEWORK! It is senseless to repeat a scene over and over, if the actor still doesn't have a basic answer to these questions. It may improve superficially, but will never interest or impact an audience in the way it should without the level of specificity provided in homework well done.

> **LIFE ACTING insists on the disciplined completion of homework and memorization before the presentation of any work.**

The choices made in homework all should be done with a sense of creativity, always thinking, "What would be the most involving and impactful choice?"

LEARN YOUR LINES!

There is no point in trying to live moment by moment, focused on getting your objective from the other actors if you are taken out of the scene because of not knowing your lines. There is no excuse. Knowing the lines and doing preliminary homework is a prerequisite for presenting any scene for rehearsal.

PROPS AND BUSINESS

One of the key components that make your character come alive is the props and stage business that the character employs. Using this can convey a lot about the character in visual shorthand. How does the character dress? Is he fastidious or slovenly? Does he move quickly or slowly? Is he regal or common in his movements? How would your character make a drink? Pack a bag? Etc. These questions are often decided with the director's input, but affect greatly the performance. Remember that all business must be tied to the intention of the character as well, and not just to illustrate the character.

EXERCISES FOR THE ACTOR

I have provided a basic primer of the LIFE ACTING model for acting. The following exercises are for the purposes of developing the instrument to better achieve the goals of LIFE ACTING. I claim no originality for these exercises.

Feedback Loop
1. Mirror exercise- two actors take the stage and face each other. No matter what happens, they are forced to imitate one another. Take turns leading. Then nobody leads.

2. "I can be hurt by you"- two actors face each other and take turns saying "I can be hurt by you" over and over.

3. Tug of War- simple exercise where two actors simulate a tug of war with no rope.

The Lines Are Not the Scenes
A. Hello

B. Hi

A. What did you do last night?

B. Not much, how about you?

A. Had a bite to eat out

B. Anything good?

A. Well no, not really.

B. See you later.

A. Ok.

Do the preceding scene as

1. A pick up scene
2. Husband and wife right after he has seen her with another man.
3. A prison conjugal visit given the one-minute warning.
4. Any situation the audience can come up with.

Emotional Life
1. Play a drunk trying to walk a straight line.
2. Play a parent giving instruction for his kids birthday party, but the kid has been diagnosed with cancer and may not live to make it.
3. Fear of sexual arousal- play trying to avoid being sexually aroused by your partner in the scene.

Characterizing Others
Perform a scene with the following choices of the others.

1. They are stupid
2. They are gods
3. They are dangerous
4. They smell
5. They are lovable
6. They want your girl
7. They are a sex object

Stage Business and Props

Do a scene while

1. Mixing a cocktail

2. Setting the table for a dinner party

3. While dressing for an occasion

4. While packing a suitcase for a trip

HOMEWORK SHEET.

Here is a sample homework sheet for you to copy and to do preliminary work in marking up your scene for presentation.

LEARN YOUR LINES!

What Do You Want from the Other Actors, and How Will You Get It?

1) **WHAT** do you want? What is the objective of this character? What is his super-objective? What are his sub-objectives in every scene, every line?

2) What do **YOU** want? What do clues from the script say about the personality of your character? What is your character's worldview? How does he see the other characters and how does he feel about them?

3) What do you **WANT**? Is your objective strong enough? Interesting enough?

4) **FROM** the other actors/characters- how can the other actors give you what you want?

5) From the other **ACTORS/CHARACTERS**- who are the other actor/characters? How do they feel about you? What do

41

they want from you? How do you feel about them?

...AND HOW ARE YOU GOING TO GET IT?

6) **HOW** are you going to get it? What tactics will you use to achieve your super-objective and sub-objectives in every line? Varied? Interesting? Imaginative?

7) How are **YOU** going to get it? What props, dress, movement, speech, makeup, would YOUR character use that would communicate his personality but also further his objective?

8) How are you going to **GET** it? Are you expecting to win, pressing in to your ideal future?

Want to see Life Acting in action? Go to lifeacting.com
Enter your email to gain free access to video training where you will see an actor improve as he puts the Life Acting into practice.

Please leave a review on Amazon if you enjoyed the book.
www.lifeacting.com
www.danieljordano.com

Printed in Great Britain
by Amazon